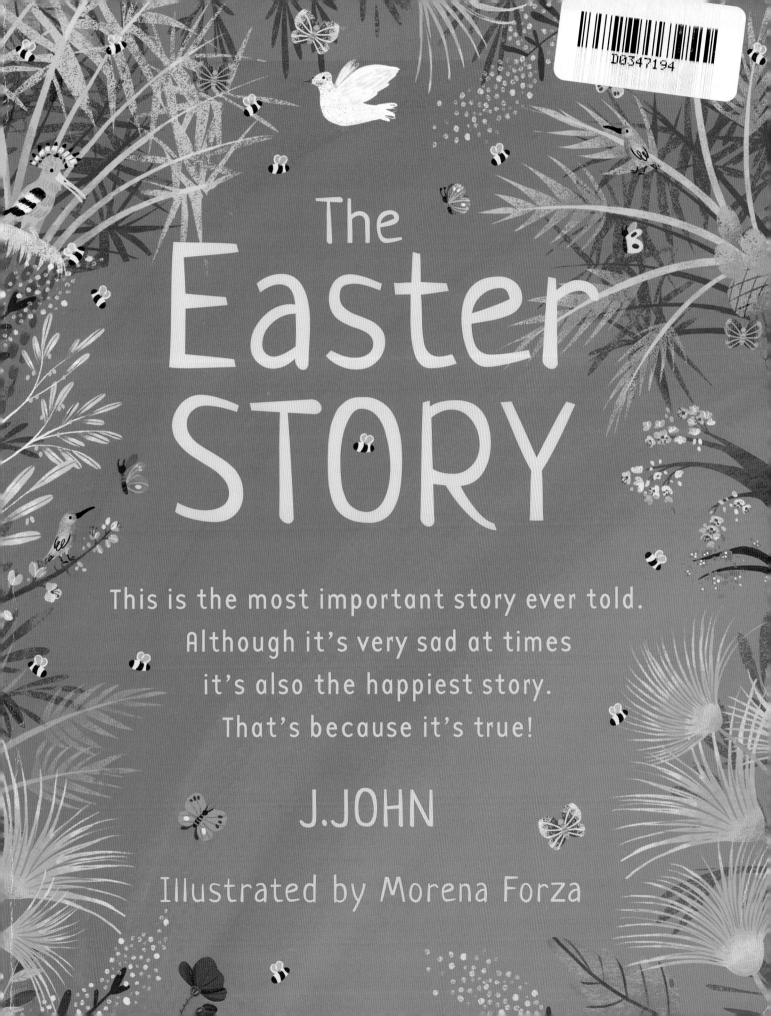

The Easter STORY

This is the most important story ever told.
Although it's very sad at times
it's also the happiest story.
That's because it's true!

J.JOHN

Illustrated by Morena Forza

D0347194

Jesus was a man who travelled around his country, Israel, two thousand years ago, teaching about God. Jesus knew God because God was his loving father.

Jesus did incredible miracles, like healing sick people, calming storms and feeding thousands of people from just five loaves of bread and two fish – that is amazing!

Jesus promised people that God's King was coming and that his kingdom was free for everybody to enter. The crowds loved Jesus, but some religious leaders didn't like what he was teaching, especially his claim to be God.

At this time the people were ruled by the Romans who were often very nasty and forced everybody to pay lots of tax (which is money you have to pay to the government). Unsurprisingly people didn't like the Romans and looked forward to the day when God's King would rescue them.

Many people followed Jesus, including twelve men who were his close friends. They are known as his disciples. One spring, after teaching for three years, Jesus and his disciples went to the city of Jerusalem for the Feast of Passover.

Passover reminded the Jewish people how God cared for them a long time ago and how he had rescued them from slavery. Because it was a feast there was a special meal to remember the agreement God had made with them when he rescued them.

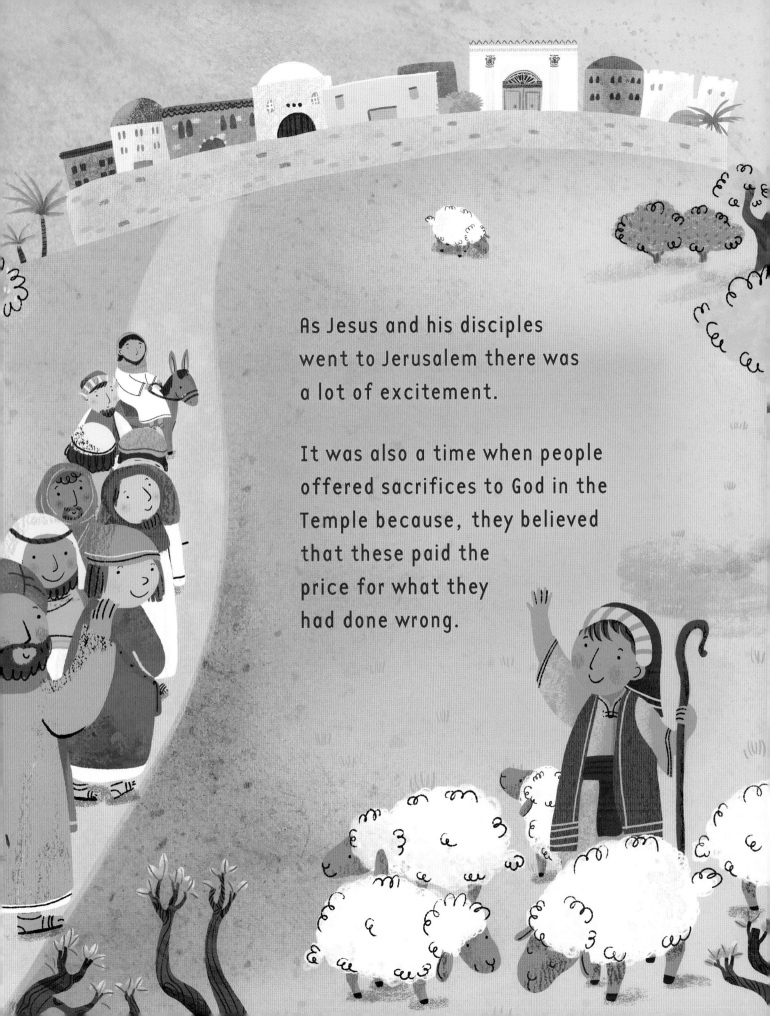

As Jesus and his disciples went to Jerusalem there was a lot of excitement.

It was also a time when people offered sacrifices to God in the Temple because, they believed that these paid the price for what they had done wrong.

Everybody, including Jesus' disciples, hoped that he was the King they were waiting for. Jesus, however, had warned his disciples that it wasn't going to be like that and that he was going to die and come back to life. The trouble was they didn't understand him.

So, when Jesus came into Jerusalem he didn't ride in as a mighty king on an impressive horse as the people expected, but instead came on a gentle donkey. People cheered but they were puzzled.

The most important place in
Jerusalem was the temple.
It was an enormous building
where sacrifices to God were
made. At its very centre was
a special room sealed off by
a great curtain.

Now although the people
knew that God was everywhere,
they believed that this room
was somewhere very special.
It was as though it was the
place where God lived.

It was such an important place
that only one man was allowed
to enter it and then just once
a year. Ordinary people, like you
and me, weren't allowed to get
anywhere near it. Not at all.

The temple should have been treated with respect but when Jesus went to see it he found it had become like a marketplace. It was full of noisy animals and people selling things to the poor and cheating them.

Jesus shouted, "You've let God's house become the home of robbers!" and told some people to get out. They didn't like that!

Over the next few days Jesus taught in Jerusalem, but many of the religious leaders wanted to get rid of him. But getting rid of Jesus wasn't easy: he was popular and Jerusalem was crowded with visitors.

Then one of Jesus' disciples, a man called Judas, came to the bad leaders. "If you pay me money," he said, "I'll show you how to catch Jesus." They agreed to his offer.

The sacrifices for Passover were made on the Friday afternoon. The evening before that, Jesus held a special meal with his twelve disciples.

He took bread and wine and told everybody that they were symbols of his death. Jesus also told his friends that he would be going away but he would send them God's Holy Spirit. "I'm going to make a new agreement between God and people," he said.

His friends didn't understand what he meant.

After the meal Jesus went out with his friends
to a quiet garden where he prayed about what
was going to happen. As he finished praying
Judas arrived with soldiers to arrest him.
Instead of staying with him, Jesus' friends
ran away. Judas realised that he had made a
terrible mistake, but by then it was too late.

Early on the Friday morning Jesus was brought in front of the religious leaders. They accused him of saying wrong things about God and of claiming to be God's King.

Finally, Jesus told them that he was indeed God's King. That made the religious leaders angry and they sent Jesus to the Roman governor, Pontius Pilate, a man who had the power to put Jesus to death.

Pontius Pilate soon decided that Jesus was innocent and should be set free, but the religious leaders and a crowd that had gathered demanded that Jesus be killed.

The Roman punishment for their enemies was crucifixion: being nailed to a cross made from pieces of wood and left to die.

Hoping that he could save Jesus from being crucified, Pilate had him beaten by the soldiers. It wasn't enough for the crowd. "Crucify him!" they shouted. In the end Pilate ordered that Jesus should be put to death.

Now the story gets as sad as any story can be. Jesus was taken away to a place where everybody could see him and he was nailed to a cross. Crowds gathered around the cross and people laughed and joked about Jesus in the cruellest way.

Where were Jesus' disciples at this horrible time? Sadly, almost all of them had run away, but some of the women who had followed him stayed to watch what happened.

As Jesus began to die, an awful darkness fell across the land. Day became night. It was as if Jesus was grabbing hold of every evil and horrible thing in the world and taking it into himself.

Finally, Jesus died. As he did, the great curtain in the temple that separated the place where God lived from everybody else was ripped apart by some invisible force. It was a sign that Jesus had made a way to God for everybody. The sacrifices and the temple were never going to be needed again.

As the sun began to set, Jesus' body was taken by a good religious leader and wrapped in cloth and taken to a private garden where he was put in a tomb that was like a cave. The tomb was closed by a big heavy stone.

Meanwhile, Pontius Pilate ordered soldiers to stand guard around the tomb in case Jesus' body was stolen.

Night fell.

Saturday was a special day of rest when nothing was allowed to happen. It came and went.

The women who followed Jesus knew that, because everything had been so rushed, Jesus' body had not been properly prepared for the grave. So early on the Sunday morning, they returned to the tomb with the special spices needed for burial. But when they got there they found, to their astonishment, that the soldiers had gone and the big heavy stone guarding the tomb had been rolled away.

Looking inside they saw that the body of Jesus was not there but instead, neatly folded, was the cloth in which Jesus had been wrapped. It all made no sense!

Then they saw an angel who told them that Jesus was no longer dead but alive.

The women ran back quickly to where Jesus' disciples were hiding and told them the news, but they found it very difficult to believe.

That Easter Sunday Jesus began appearing to his disciples and followers. At first they found it hard to believe but soon realised there could be no doubt that Jesus was really alive again.

It was certainly Jesus because he still had the scars on his hands from being nailed to the cross. And he was really alive because they could talk to him, touch him and eat with him.

It was very exciting news because Jesus had fought with death and defeated it.

For forty days Jesus spoke with his disciples and followers. He turned up in rooms and on roads. He appeared to men and women and on one occasion to hundreds of people.

During this time Jesus explained to his followers that God's King needed to die in order to be the sacrifice for the wrong things that we have all done. But because he was innocent, death hadn't been able to keep hold of him. Jesus was now the King who could give eternal life to those who trusted him.

As Jesus said, "I am the way, the truth and the life."

Jesus also told his followers that they were to share this good news about him with the whole world and that wherever they went he would always be with them. He promised that one day he would come back from heaven to earth and make everything in the world new and right.

Finally Jesus met with his followers and told them it was time for him to return to heaven. With those words he rose into the sky and disappeared from sight.

Jesus is God's King and we can know him and know that he will be with us for ever. Pray this prayer if you would like to know Jesus:

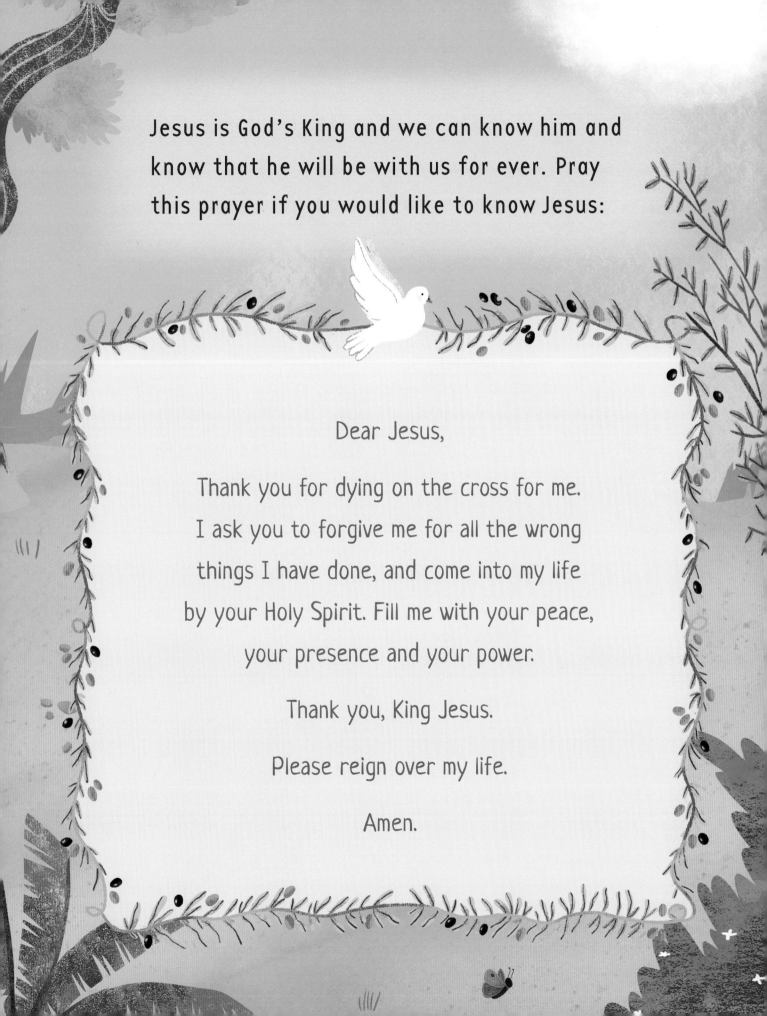

Dear Jesus,

Thank you for dying on the cross for me. I ask you to forgive me for all the wrong things I have done, and come into my life by your Holy Spirit. Fill me with your peace, your presence and your power.

Thank you, King Jesus.

Please reign over my life.

Amen.

Finally, let me encourage you.
I made a decision to follow Jesus
forty-two years ago. It has not always
been easy but it is the best decision
I have ever made. Living my life as a friend
of God through Jesus has been an amazing
adventure. And I pray it will be an
amazing adventure for you too.

J.JOHN